101
things
to make
and do

This is a Parragon Publishing book
This edition published in 2006

Parragon
Queen Street House
4 Queen Street
Bath BA1 1HE, UK

Copyright © Parragon Books Ltd 2006

ISBN 1-40547-126-3
Printed in China

101
things
to make
and do

p

Contents

GREAT GIFTS

TOYS and GAMES

SPECIAL OCCASIONS

Measurements and recipes

Follow these recipes for perfect papier-mâché and super salt dough. Use them for the projects in this book or create your own masterpieces!

Papier-mâché

Papier-mâché is perfect for making all kinds of models. There are lots of different recipes, but this is the easiest.

You will need:

✦ Newspaper, torn into short strips.

✦ Dish of white glue, mixed with an equal amount of water (you can add a little wallpaper paste if you like).

✦ Old paintbrush.

Paint the strips of paper with glue on both sides, using a paintbrush. Place the strips one at a time over the object to be covered and smooth them down with your hands. Add one layer at a time. Don't put too many on at once or it will take too long to dry.

You can make a bowl either by covering a balloon (p.58) or wrapping layers around a real bowl. If you do this, smear petroleum jelly over the bowl before you start, so the model will slip off easily when it's dry.

Salt dough

This recipe will make enough salt dough for the basket on p.52.

You will need:

- ¾ cup plain flour
- 3 tbsp salt
- 1 teaspoon cooking oil
- ⅓ cup water
- Mixing bowl
- Board

Mix together the flour, salt, and cooking oil in a bowl using your fingers. Add a little water and mix it in thoroughly until you have a smooth and thick dough dry enough not to stick to the sides of the bowl. If your mixture is too sticky, simply add more flour. If it's too crumbly, add water.

Sprinkle a little flour over the board and knead the dough on it until it is a smooth lump. You can store the dough in a sealed container in the fridge for a couple of days.

Bake in a preheated oven at 250°F for about three hours until firm. Baking times will vary depending on the size and thickness of your object, but make sure it's hard all through.

Oven temperatures

Centigrade	Fahrenheit
120	250
150	300
180	350
200	400
230	450

Get crafty!

Here's the inside facts on the best materials to use, and ways to save your hard-earned pocket money by becoming a crafty collector.

Essentials

It's a good idea to keep all your craft materials together. You could design your own craft box.

Here's a useful list of the things you'll need to do most of the projects in this book. And don't forget—birthdays and Christmas are useful times to ask for that special set of paints you can't afford to buy yourself.

◆ A set of acrylic or poster paints and brushes
◆ Colored pencils and felt-tipped pens
◆ A pot of white glue and an old brush
◆ Scissors—the ones with rounded ends are the safest.
◆ Black fine-tipped fiber pen
◆ Pencil, ruler, and an eraser for those little mistakes.

Materials

There are some things you have to buy, but you can recycle or go hunting for lots of stuff. See how good you can get at finding craft materials for free. It's really fun!

Saving paper

No more ripping wrapping off presents. A crafty collector saves wrapping paper. If it's very crumpled, get an adult to iron it with a cool iron, and it will be as good as new.

Cardboard

Cardboard comes in different thicknesses. Often, you can use recycled cardboard instead of buying it, so save all your cereal and laundry detergent boxes. Large objects often delivered in cardboard boxes, so keep an eye out for it.

Fabric

Have you grown out of your favorite jeans? Don't worry! You can recycle them. Denim can be turned into bags, purses, pencil cases—the list is endless! Save scraps of patterned fabric too. They can be used to decorate your creations.

Odds and ends

The crafty collector knows that buttons and beads make great decorations. You can make monster eyes from buttons and jewellery from beads. Even bottle tops come in handy!

Nature trail

When you're outside, you'll come across all kinds of things to add to your collection. Pick up leaves, twigs, feathers, and seed heads in the park and collect flowers from the garden to dry, but ask first before you pick any prize blooms! At the beach, look for interesting pebbles and shells for your collection.

9

Mosaic boat scene

Do you feel like a change from painting your favorite pictures? Stick colored scraps of paper onto your drawing instead, for a colorful mosaic effect.

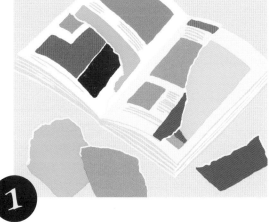

You Will Need

+ Old magazines
+ Scissors
+ 8 x 11 inch sheet of white paper and pencil
+ White glue
+ Brush
+ Large square of blue paper

1 Choose colored sections of old magazines. Tear out scraps of green and blue for the sea and sky, bright shades for the sails, and dark shades for the boats.

2 Cut the scraps into squares of roughly the same size, about $1/2$ inch.

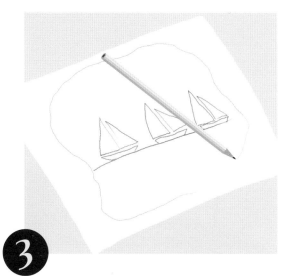

3 Lightly draw a seaside scene on the white paper. Draw a wavy line around the picture, as a guide to where to finish sticking squares.

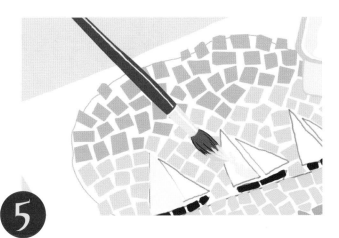

4 Start placing the squares onto your picture. When you are happy with the design, glue the squares down.

5 Make triangles to fit roughly into the sail shapes. Cut around the picture, then glue it to a larger square of blue paper.

Leave space between the squares when you stick them down.

Piggy bookmark

This piggy bookmark will help you keep your place next time you read a book.

You Will Need

- Strip of cardboard or thick paper 1 1/2 x 8 inches
- Scrap of pink cardboard or thick paper 2 3/4 inches square
- Pencil
- Scissors
- White glue
- 2 stick-on google eyes
- Black felt-tipped pen

1 Draw the outline of a pig's face and two trotters on the pink cardboard. Cut out the pig shape.

2 Stick on the google eyes using the white glue.

3 Using the black pen, draw around the nose and mouth, then add nostrils and ear creases. Color the trotters black.

4 Glue the pig face to the strip of card. Make the head stick up about 1 inch over the top of the strip. Leave it to dry.

Give your bookmarks a fluffy touch by gluing a few threads of wool to the faces.

Try This!

Animal Farm

Make a colorful collection of animal bookmarks for all your favorite books. It's a great way to use up leftover strips of cardboard from other projects. Try a pony, a cute cat, a dog, or even a penguin.

Paper airplanes

These simple paper gliders have a clever secret to make them fly brilliantly. With a bit of practice, you can even make them loop through the air!

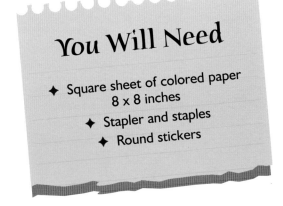

You Will Need

✦ Square sheet of colored paper 8 x 8 inches
✦ Stapler and staples
✦ Round stickers

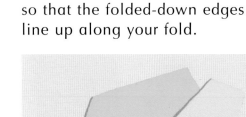

1 Fold the sheet of paper in half. Turn down the corners at one end so that the folded-down edges line up along your fold.

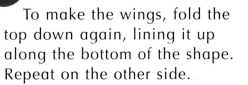

2 To make the wings, fold the top down again, lining it up along the bottom of the shape. Repeat on the other side.

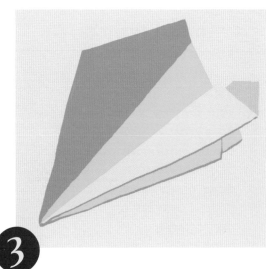

3 Fold the top flaps down again, lining them up along the bottom of the airplane.

14

Try This!

Floating glider

There are lots of variations of planes to try—this glider floats gently to earth like a seedpod from a tree. You can adjust the angles of the wings to make it loop in midair.

4

Open out the folds that you made in the last step. To help the plane fly better, puy two staples in the folded layers near the nose. Decorate the plane with round stickers on the wings and sides.

The triangular flaps at the wing bases will make the plane fly in different directions. Fold them up for an inside loop and down for an outside loop.

Top Tip

Your plane will fly much better if you fold really carefully. Line up each fold exactly before making the crease.

Groovy gift bag

If you have a gift that's an odd shape and difficult to wrap neatly, why not make this gift bag for it instead? It's really simple!

1 Brush glue on the white paper and stick the tissue paper to it. Then glue the wrapping paper to the other side of the white paper. Cut the glued sheets to 45 x 30cm.

You Will Need

- 11 x 8 inch sheet orange tissue paper
- 1 sheet patterned gift wrapping paper
- 11 x 8 inch sheet of white paper
- Ruler and pencil
- White glue and brush
- ½ yard red ribbon, ¾ inch wide
- 10 inch pink ribbon, ½ inch wide

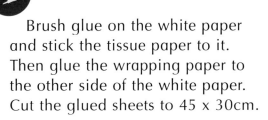

2 Draw two lines, from the top and bottom of the sheet. Then draw two lines in from the sides. Fold and unfold along the lines to make creases.

Small tab   Long tab

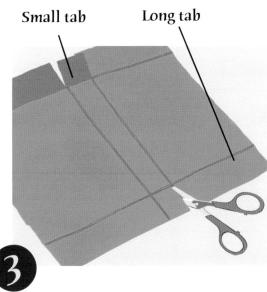

3 Use scissors to cut four slits up to where the lines cross, to make small and long tabs. Fold the two small tabs in.

16

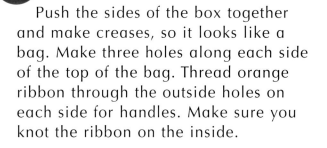

◀ This part is easier than it sounds! Paste glue along the four long tabs. Lift up the paper until edges A and B meet. Press the long tabs together then reach inside and pull up the small tags, gluing them to the sides. You wll now have a box shape.

5 Push the sides of the box together and make creases, so it looks like a bag. Make three holes along each side of the top of the bag. Thread orange ribbon through the outside holes on each side for handles. Make sure you knot the ribbon on the inside.

6 Once you have put your gift in the bag, thread the pink ribbon through the middle holes and tie it in a bow.

Paper poppies

These poppies look very realistic, especially when light shines through the crêpe-paper petals.

You Will Need

For each poppy:
+ Crêpe paper in red, light green, and dark green
+ Scissors
+ 2 pieces green garden wire
+ 20 small black beads
+ Black felt
+ White glue and brush
+ Zig-zag scissors

1 Cut out six circles from the red crêpe, about 3 inches diameter. Pull gently on each circle to stretch them into a dish shape.

2 Twist the tip of the garden wire and thread 20 black beads onto it. Twist the beaded wire into a tight spiral shape.

◄ Using the zig-zag scissors, cut out a 2-inch circle from the black felt. Stack the paper disks loosely on top of one another with the felt circle on top. Poke the nonbeaded end of the wire through the center and pull it through.

3

◄ Cut ¼ inch strips of dark green paper and paste them with white glue. Stick the top of the strip to the back of the flower and wind it all the way down the wire. Wrap a shorter piece of wire in the same way.

4

Try This!

Posy of pansies
Make these pansies in the same way, using lilac crêpe paper. Cut a figure-eight from the black felt and thread the wire with a single yellow bead to make the flowers' centers.

5

Twist the two pieces of wire together to make a stem and leaf. Using the zig-zag scissors, cut a leaf shape from the light green crêpe and glue it to the underside of the leaf stem.

Bubble-print gift wrap

All you need for this bubbly gift is washing up liquid, paints and plenty of puff! Use the idea to make matching gift tags and cards, too.

You Will Need

✦ Old newspapers
✦ Ready mixed paints: red, blue
✦ Washing-up liquid
✦ Water
✦ Old spoon
✦ Drinking straws
✦ Shallow bowl
✦ White paper

1 Cover the work surface with newspaper sheets; this is a messy project! Using an old spoon, stir together ½ cup water, 1-2 tablespoons red paint, and ½ tablespoon washing-up liquid in the bowl.

2 Put a straw in the paint mixture and gently blow to make bubbles. Keep blowing until the bubbles are almost over the edge of the dish.

3 Put a piece of paper on top of the bubbles and hold it there until several bubbles have popped. Move the paper and continue popping bubbles until most of the paper has been printed.

4 Clean the bowl and make a blue paint mixture. Repeat steps 1 to 3 so you have a blue and red bubbly pattern. Leave the paper to dry.

Top Tip

If you don't get enough bubbles when you blow, add a drop more washing up liquid. If the bubbles are too faint on the paper, add more paint to the mixture.

Printed star card

Make your own stamps for cards. Try stars as shown, or experiment with your own ideas.

You Will Need

✦ Sheet of blue card 300 x 150mm, folded in half
✦ Tracing paper and pencil
✦ 3 pieces funky foam 50 x 50mm
✦ 3 pieces thick card 50 x 50mm
✦ Scissors
✦ Poster paints: red, yellow, dark blue and brush
✦ White glue
✦ Red glitter

1 Stick a foam square onto a square of card. Add yellow paint to your stamp and print it in one corner of the card. Print four more squares in the corners and middle of the card. Leave to dry.

2 Meanwhile, trace a star, using the template on p92. Transfer it onto the foam and cut out two stars. Stick each star to squares of thick card.

3 Add blue paint to one of the star stamps and print a star onto each blue square, pressing down firmly.

4 Use the other star stamp to print red stars on the yellow squares. Leave the card to dry.

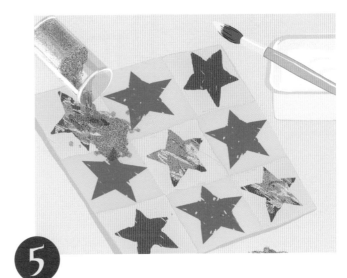

5 Dilute a little PVA glue with water and brush it onto the middle, top left and bottom right red stars. Sprinkle red glitter over the glued stars and shake off the excess glitter. Leave to dry.

Try This!

Gift tag

Make a matching gift tag by folding a piece of card 4 x 2 inches in half and stamping each side. Finish by making a hole and threading through some red ribbon.

Dinosaur mail holder

An armor-plated stegosaurus is just what you need to keep your important cards and letters from escaping!

1 Trace the templates on p.93 onto purple cardboard. Cut out two dinosaur shapes and two bases. Trace the face and neck onto one of the dinosaur shapes.

2 Trace the armor plates onto orange paper. Cut them out, making them a little smaller than your outline. Glue them, one at a time, along the spine of the dinosaur, leaving a border around each shape.

3 Glue on the googly eyes and go over the face and mouth with a black felt-tipped pen.

4 Cover the body shapes with yellow stick-on dots.

5 Cut out four legs in each dinosaur shape. Cut two slots in the base shapes. Slot the shapes together so that you make a holderfor your mail.

Racing yachts

These great little yachts are made from corks, and no matter what you do, they'll never sink. Try it and see!

You Will Need

For each yacht:
- ✦ 3 corks
- ✦ All-purpose glue
- ✦ 2 popsiclesticks
- ✦ Toothpick
- ✦ Scraps of colored paper

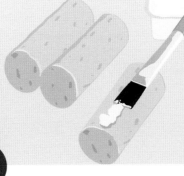

1 Glue the three corks together, side by side, using the strong glue. Leave to dry.

2 Glue the two popsiclesticks to the top of the corks as shown. Leave to dry.

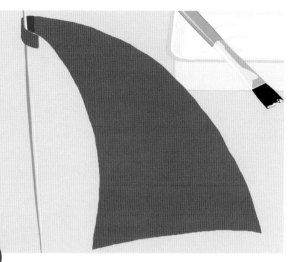

3 While the glue is drying, cut a triangular sail from one of the scraps of colored paper. Apply a little glue to the tip of the sail and wrap it around the top of the toothpick. Leave to dry.

4 Make a hole in the center of the middle cork between the sticks. Push the toothpick mast firmly into the hole. Bend the sail round so it sits on the top of the boat.

5 Cut a tiny triangle in yellow paper and glue to the top of the toothpick mast to make a flag.

Try This!

One-cork yacht

If you don't have lots of corks, make a simpler version using just one. Push three map tacks in a row along the bottom of the cork to help your yacht stay upright.

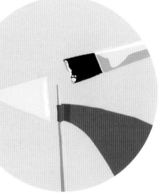

Blazing sneakers

Use fabric paint straight from the tube to make flaming streaks and a scary skull design on your slip-on sneakers. They'll help you run like the blazes!

You Will Need

+ Pair of black slip-on sneakers
+ Relief fabric paints: white, red, orange, and yellow

1 Use the white paint to draw a skull outline on the front of each shoe. Then fill in the skulls, leaving circles for the eye sockets and a double row of teeth.

2 With the red paint, draw flames on either side of the skulls. Fill in the bottom of the flames in red and leave to dry.

3 Use the orange paint to fill in the middle part of each flame and leave to dry.

4 Finish by filling in the last sections using the yellow paint. Leave the sneakers to dry.

Try This!

Party shoes

If you prefer a pretty princess look, stick on gems and use fabric relief pens to cover ballet slippers in a dotted flower pattern.

To Tip

Sometimes the paint shrinks a little as it dries. Simply wait until the paint has dried completely then touch in some fresh paint.

29

Striped money box

Save your spare coins in a cool striped money bank made from a lidded cardboard container. Take the lid off to make a pencil holder.

You Will Need

✦ Empty cardboard container with lid
✦ Ruler and pencil
✦ 11 x 8 inch sheets of colored paper
✦ White glue and brush
✦ Craft knife or scalpel

1

Measure the height of the container and cut the paper to the same height. Draw lines down one of the sheets, changing the distance between the lines to make narrower and wider stripes.

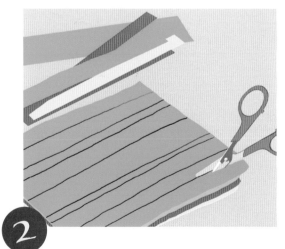

2

Put the ruled sheet with the lines drawn on it on top of the others and cut along the lines to make long strips.

3

Paste the strips with glue and stick them to the box, making sure they overlap and smoothing them down carefullly.

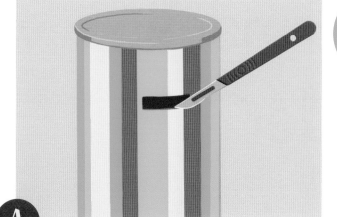

4

When the glue has dried, ask an adult to cut a money slot measuring about 2 x ¼ inches.

Try This!

Extra safe

If you're always raiding your money bank, make this no-lid version from a granola bar box. Use parcel tape to seal it, then decorate it with the paper strips. You'll have to break the whole box to get your hands on the cash!

Papier-mâché CD holder

Granola bar boxes are perfect to make this groovy CD holder, so get munching!

You Will Need

✦ 4 identical empty cardboard granola bar boxes
✦ Scissors
✦ White glue
✦ Masking tape
✦ Thick cardboard
✦ Torn newspaper pieces
✦ Paints: white, silver
✦ Brush
✦ 3 old CDs

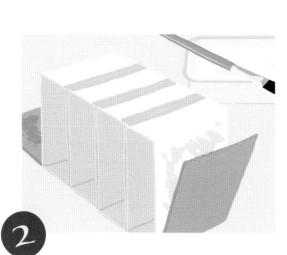

1

◀ Cut the lids off of all the boxes. Glue the boxes in a row and add masking tape along the joins.

2

Cut out two squares of thick cardboard the same size as the box sides, and glue one to each end of the boxes.

3

Make papier-mâché mix following the recipe on p6. Apply a layer of newspaper all over the outside and around the edges of the boxes.

4 When the papier-mâché is dry, paint the boxes white all over. Leave to dry.

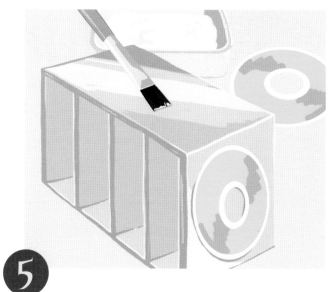

5 Paint the outside silver. When it is dry, glue a CD on each end and on the top.

Yogurt carton herb garden

These cartons, planted with scrumptious herbs, will look great in the kitchen window. Don't forget to water them!

You Will Need

✦ 3 yogurt cartons
✦ Sandpaper
✦ Acrylic paints: red, green, yellow, white
✦ 3 jar lids
✦ Potted herbs: basil, oregano, chives
✦ Soil mix
✦ Awl or screwdriver

1 Wash and dry the cartons and rub all over the outsides with sandpaper. This will help paint to stay on the pots.

2 Get an adult to help with this part. Make holes in the bottom of each pot with an awl or screwdriver.

3 Paint two coats on the outside of the pots: one each of yellow, green, and red. When the paint has dried, dab white dots on each pot.

4 Paint some jar lids to make matching saucers.

5 Carefully remove the herbs from their pots and replant them. Add extra soil mix to fill the pots. Press it down and water the herbs well.

To Tip

Herbs taste great. Try adding fresh basil to tomato pasta sauce. Oregano is perfect for pizza, and minced chives are delicious sprinkled on top of creamy potato salad.

Denim phone holder

Never throw your old jeans away. You can turn them into all kinds of useful stuff, such as this cool cellphone holder.

You Will Need

✦ Old peice of denim
✦ Zig-zag scissors
✦ Red wool: 3½ inch pieces
✦ Needle and red thread
✦ Button
✦ Fabric glue
✦ Scrap of red felt
✦ Scissors
✦ Craft knife

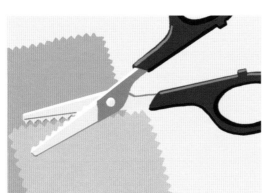

1 Cut the denim to 12 x 4 inches using zig-zag scissors. Fold the fabric, leaving a flap at the top.

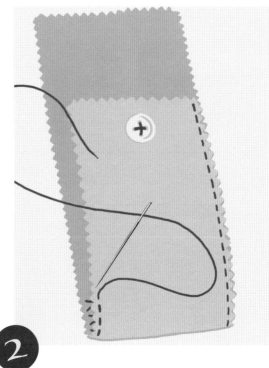

2 Use a needle and red thread to sew up each side of the holder. Sew a small button onto the front.

Make a braided string. Put the three lengths of red wool together and tie a knot at one end. Braid the strands together and knot the other end. Stitch the braid to either side of the holder.

Cut out butterfly shapes from the red felt. Fold over the top flap and glue a butterfly over where you can feel the button underneath. Glue the other butterfly at the bottom of the bag.

Ask an adult to cut a slit in the top butterfly to make a buttonhole.

Fruit smoothies

Ask an adult to help with the chopping, then whisk yourself a delicious, healthy fruit drink!

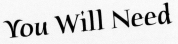

You Will Need

For the strawberry smoothie:

✦ 4 strawberries
✦ $\frac{2}{3}$ cup sliced mango
✦ 1 small banana
✦ Juice of 1 orange
✦ 3 tbsp yogurt
✦ 1 tbsp honey
✦ Hand blender with pot
✦ Glass and straws

1 Chop three strawberries, the mango and the banana. Put them in the bowl with all the other other ingredients.

2 Blend everything until you have a smooth, runny mixture.

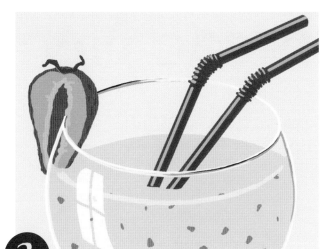

3

Pour the smoothie mixture into a glass. Cut the remaining strawberry in half and use it to decorate the glass. Add colorful straws.

Try This!

Frozen treats

Why not make delicious fruit smoothie frozen? Just pour the smoothie mixture into a tray, add a stick, and put it in the freezer!

This yummy smoothie was made with mango and pineapple.

If you prefer a sharper taste, go for fruits of the forest. You can buy frozen packages in the supermarket.

Gingerbread Men

If you want to make this project even more quickly, buy an icing pen. Try other shapes, too, such as animals and vehicles.

1 Heat the butter and sugar gently in a pan until the sugar dissolves and the butter melts.

You Will Need

- ✦ 2 tbsp butter
- ✦ 1/2 cup brown sugar
- ✦ 4 tbsp molasses
- ✦ 1 cup plus 2 tbsp all-purpose flour
- ✦ Pinch of salt
- ✦ 1/2 tbsp each baking powder, ginger, cinammon
- ✦ Gingerbread man cutter
- ✦ Rolling pin, cookie sheet, sieve, bowl, saucepan
- ✦ **Icing**: 1/2 cup confectioner's sugar, water, blue food coloring, waxed paper sandwich bag.

2 Sift all the other ingredients into a large bowl. Add the melted mixture and mix it all together until you have a soft ball of dough. Put it in the fridge for an hour.

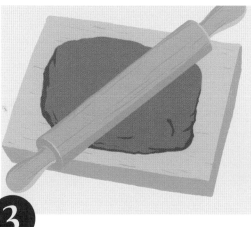

3 Roll the dough out to about 3/4 inch thick.

4 Use the cutter to make shapes in the dough. Put them on a greased cookie sheet and bake them at 375°F for five minutes.

5 While the cookies cool, make the icing. Sift confectioner's sugar into a bowl, add a few drops of blue food color and a little water, and mix until you have a thick paste.

6 When the cookies are cold, snip the corner off of a paper bag and spoon the icing in. Decorate your gingerbread man by squeezing the bag gently so that the icing comes out of the snipped corner.

Pirate treasure map

This battered map looks as if it has crossed the seven seas and been hidden down a pirate's pantaloons. But will it lead you to hidden treasure?

You Will Need

✦ Sheet of thick construction paper
✦ Bowl of warm water
✦ Instant coffee granules
✦ Paper towels
✦ Felt-tipped pens

1 Tear the edges from all around your sheet of paper to give it rough edges.

◄ Crumple the sheet of paper up into a ball so that it is really creased.

2

◄ Flatten the paper and dip it into a bowl of warm water. Put the wet paper on the draining board and sprinkle over a spoonful of coffee granules. Leave for a few minutes.

3

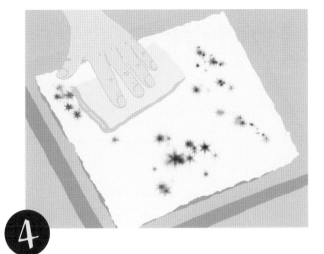

4 Dab the stains with paper towels then dip the paper in a bowl of warm water. Repeat the staining and rinsing on the other side of the paper. Leave it to dry out.

5 Draw a treasure map like the one shown. Add dangerous areas with a skull and crossbones and mark the hidden treasure with a big X.

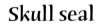

Try This!

Skull seal

To keep your map secret, roll it up and tie it with ribbon. Add a scary skull and crossbones seal made from modeling clay.

Fishy burgers

Everyone will love these delicious, healthy burgers. If you like vegetarian food, mash up a can of kidney beans and use them instead of the salmon.

You Will Need

To make 4 burgers:

- ✦ I small onion, chopped
- ✦ Pinch of mixed herbs
- ✦ A large handful of breadcrumbs
- ✦ 8 ounce can of red salmon
- ✦ I egg
- ✦ Salt and pepper
- ✦ A little flour
- ✦ Skillet and a little oil
- ✦ Lettuce, tomotoes, onion rings, mayonnaise
- ✦ Burger bun

1 Ask an adult to help with the cooking. Heat the oil in the skillet add the onion, herbs, and breadcrumbs and cook gently for 5 minutes.

2 ◀ Pour the mixture into a bowl and add the salmon, egg and a little salt and pepper. Mix everything together with your hands.

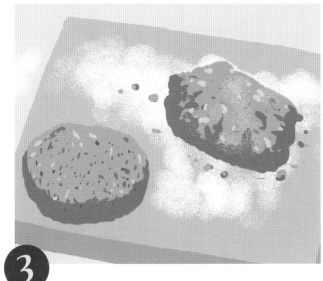

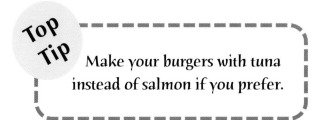

Top Tip Make your burgers with tuna instead of salmon if you prefer.

3 Sprinkle some flour onto a work surface and shape the mixture into burger shapes, using clean hands.

4 Wash and dry the skillet, add a little more oil, and place over medium heat. Fry the burger for five minutes on each side.

5 Put each burger on a bun and garnish with lettuce, tomatoes, onion rings, and mayonnaise.

45

Printed T-shirt

Do you think vegetables are yucky? Think again! They are perfect for making prints. Try this froggy T-shirt and see for yourself.

1 Ask an adult to help with this part. Cut the two potatoes in half and trim the top of the celery. Cut a 1 ¼ inch piece of carrot; then cut it in half lengthways.

You Will Need

- ✦ T-shirt
- ✦ Piece of scrap cardboard
- ✦ Vegetables: I large and I small potato, I stalk of celery, I carrot
- ✦ Cutting board and knife
- ✦ Green fabric paint
- ✦ Shallow dish
- ✦ Tube of fabric relief paint: metallic blue

2 Put a scrap of cardboard inside the shirt to stop the paint from seeping through. Pour some of the green paint into the dish. Dip a larger potato half into the paint, dab off any excess on the side of the plate, and make a print in the center of the T-shirt. This will be the body of the frog.

3 Use one of the small potato halves to print the two back legs. Dip the top end of the celery stalk into the paint and use to print a bulging eye. Repeat for the other eye.

4 Use the carrot to print the lower back legs and the front legs, then cut the carrot piece in half to print the front and back feet. Leave to dry.

5 Dab tiny spots all over the frog, using the tube of fabric paint. Leave the T-shirt to dry.

Try This!

Green gecko
Once you've got the hang of veggie printing, try different designs. This cute gecko was also made with potato, carrot, and celery, with yellow relief paint dotted over its body.

Cress caterpillar

If you get tired of waiting for plants to grow, cress is the answer because it only takes a few days! It tastes great in salads and sandwiches, too.

1 Take five clean, empty egg shells with their tops lopped off. Trim the tops with nail scissors.

You Will Need

- 5 egg shells
- Nail scissors
- Paints: green, red, black
- Goggle eyes
- Paintbrush
- White glue
- Packet of cress seeds
- Cotton batting
- Red pipe cleaner

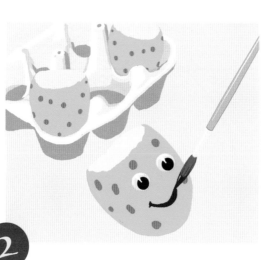

2 Paint the eggs green with red spots. Glue goggle eyes to one of them and paint a black mouth. Put them in an egg carton to dry.

3 When they are dry, put a wad of cotton batting in the bottom of each egg, add 1tsp of cress seeds, then pour a spoonful of water over the cotton batting.

48

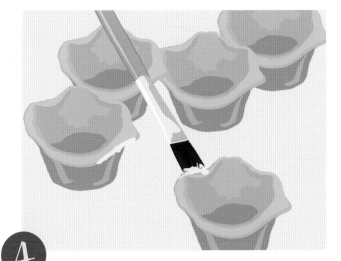

4 Cut up a cardboard egg carton to make five little dishes. Paint them green and glue them together in a wiggly line.

5 Put an egg in each dish, with the face at the front. To make antenna, twist a pipe cleaner into spirals at both ends, fold it in half, and push it into the shell with the face.

Top Tip Cress care
Don't let the cotton batting dry out. Add a little water every other day. The cress takes about a week to grow, then just snip it, wash it, and enjoy!

Pasta jewelery

Pasta comes in so many shapes and sizes that you can make a different necklace for every outfit!

1 Paint the pasta wheels in green, blue, and purple acrylic paint.

You Will Need

- ✦ Dried pasta shapes: 6 wheels, 24 curly macaroni
- ✦ Acrylic paints: green, blue, purple, gold
- ✦ Lump of plasticine
- ✦ Toothpicks
- ✦ Colored stiff elastic or cord

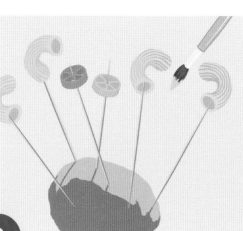

2 Paint the macaroni gold, and put all the shapes on the ends of toothpicks stuck in plasticine to dry.

Tie a button to the thread while you thread the shapes to stop them from falling off!

3 Thread three macaronis then a wheel onto the colored thread. Repeat this until all the jewels are threaded.

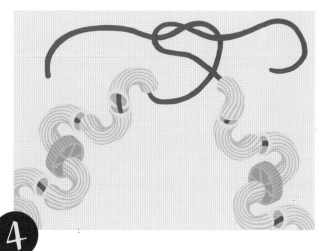

Try This!

Lots of choice
Your local supermarket has lots of different-shaped pastas, so go shopping for some inspiration!

4 Knot the two ends of the thread together, making sure you have made your necklace big enough to go over your head.

Salt-dough basket

If you don't have any clay, you can create your own! Salt dough is cheap and easy to make and can be used for all kinds of modeling projects.

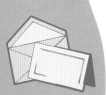

1 Sprinkle flour on the salt dough and roll it out to about $3/4$ inch thick. Use a plastic knife to cut 15 strips.

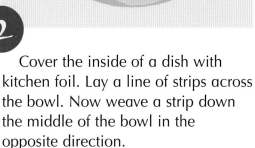

2 Cover the inside of a dish with kitchen foil. Lay a line of strips across the bowl. Now weave a strip down the middle of the bowl in the opposite direction.

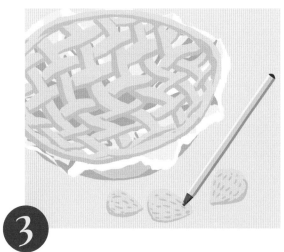

3 Carry on weaving strips to make a basket. Press a thin strip of dough all around the rim. Make strawberries from leftover dough, then poke holes in them with an old pen.

4 Bake the basket and fruit in the oven according to the instructions on p7. When they are cold, separate the dish from the basket. Paint the basket blue and the strawberries red with green dots.

5 Cut stalk shapes from the green felt and glue them to the tops of the strawberries. Then glue the strawberries to the edge of the basket.

GREAT GIFTS

Felt beads

This project is amazingly easy. Just roll up and glue colored squares of felt, then cut slices to make unusual spiral-patterned beads.

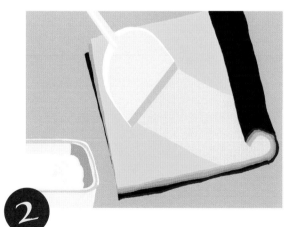

You Will Need

+ Felt squares, 3 x 3 inches: yellow, pink, and black
+ White glue
+ Scissors
+ 2 rubber bands
+ Needle and gold thread
+ 18 small black beads

1 Spread glue thinly onto the black square and stick the pink square on top. Now spread glue onto the pink square and stick the yellow square to it.

2 Spread glue thinly onto the yellow square and roll up the layers to make a swiss-roll shape.

54

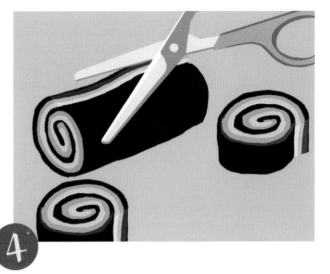

3
Hold the roll in place with a rubber band at each end and leave it to dry.

4
Remove the rubber bands and cut the roll into slices about $1/2$ inch wide. Choose the best five beads for your necklace.

5
Tie a knot in the gold thread about 4 inches from the end. Thread on three black beads, then push the needle through the top of one of the felt beads near the join. Thread three more black beads, then the next felt bead. Carry on until you have used all the beads. Tie a knot in the thread and trim the end.

Try This!

Pink pendant
Make a pendant by gluing three felt beads together. Thread beads on as shown. Push the needle through the top of your trio of beads.

Silhouette hanging

This moonlit woodland scene is made from acetate and cardboard, but it looks just like stained glass!

You Will Need

- ✦ Pair of compasses
- ✦ 3 8 x 11 inch sheets of black cardboard
- ✦ Blue acetate film
- ✦ Scissors
- ✦ Pencil
- ✦ White glue and brush
- ✦ Hole punch

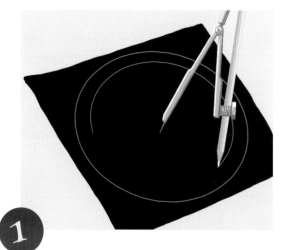

1 Use the compasses to make an 8-inch circle on the black card. Draw another circle ¾ inch from the first.

2 Cut out the ring shape, draw round it onto the other piece of card and cut that one out too. Now you have two black rings.

▶ On another piece of black cardboard draw the outlines of a grassy bank, a tree, two rabbits, a bird, and a full moon. Cut them all out.

③

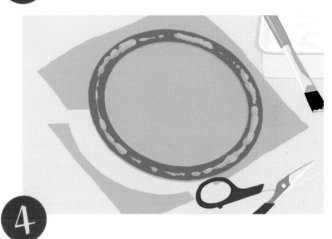

④ Brush glue around one ring and glue the acetate to it, trimming to fit the ring.

Top Tip Thread some cord through the tab and hang your picture by a window. The sun will shine through it and really make it glow.

⑤ Glue all the shapes onto the acetate. Cut out a black cardboard tab shape, make a hole in it with the hole punch, and glue it to the top of the black ring. Glue the other black ring on top of the acetate.

Papier-mâché bowl

Balloons are great for making bowls. After the papier-mâché dries, just pop the balloon to leave a perfect bowl shape!

You Will Need

- ✦ Balloon
- ✦ Torn newspaper pieces
- ✦ White glue and water
- ✦ Scissors
- ✦ Masking tape
- ✦ Round plastic bendy lid
- ✦ White latex paint and brush
- ✦ Ruler and pencil
- ✦ Set of acrylic paints
- ✦ Water-based varnish and brush

1 Blow up the balloon. Make the papier-mâché mix using the recipe on p.6. Paste a layer of newspaper strips halfway up the balloon. Repeat with three more layers.

2 When it is dry, pop the balloon and remove it. Trim the edges of the bowl by cutting round the rim.

3 Sit the bowl in the plastic lid and tape them together. Paste two more layers of papier-mâché over the whole model and leave it to dry.

4 Paint the pot all over, including the inside, with a coat of white latex paint. Leave to dry. Hold the ruler up beside the pot and mark two straight lines of dots around the bowl. Join the dots to make lines.

5 Paint on a striped pattern in bright colors and leave to dry. Add spots, triangles, and black outlines. Leave to dry, then add a thin coat of varnish to make the bowl tough and shiny.

Copy this colorful design or make up a pattern of your own.

Top Tip It's important to leave papier-mâché to dry before you pop the balloon or start painting. If it is still soft and damp, you could easily put your finger through it!

Kitty photo album

This collage photo album makes a purr-fect present for your favourite cat lover! Adapt it to make a great scrapbook, too.

You Will Need

- ✦ 6 sheets 11 x 8 inch colored cardboard
- ✦ Scraps of card in orange, white, pink, green, black, and blue
- ✦ Hole punch
- ✦ Pinking shears
- ✦ White glue
- ✦ 1 yard piece of green cord

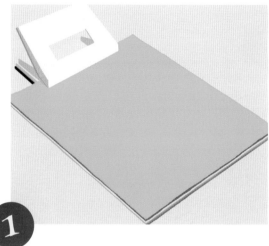

1 Pile together the six sheets of colored cardboard with cover sheet on top. Punch two holes on the left-hand side.

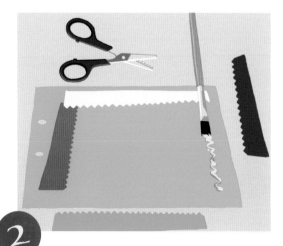

2 Cut a strip each from the card scraps, using the pinking shears. Arrange them to make a border on the cover and glue in place.

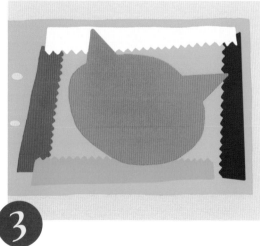

3 Draw and cut out a large cat face from orange cardboard. Stick it on the cover, overlapping the borders as shown.

4

Draw and cut out the cat's features: oval white eyes with green and black pupils. A pink nose, mouth, and ears, and black whiskers. Arrange these on the face and glue them in place.

5

Thread the length of cord through the holes, starting from the back and including all the pages. Tie in a bow at the front. Knot the ends of the cord to stop them from fraying.

GREAT GIFTS

Flowery earrings

It's really easy to make jewelery with oven-bake clay and it comes in so many colors you'll never run out of ideas.

You Will Need

- ✦ Oven-bake clay: red, yellow, blue
- ✦ Rolling pin
- ✦ Plastic sheet or tablecloth
- ✦ Plastic knife
- ✦ Earring backs
- ✦ All-purpose glue

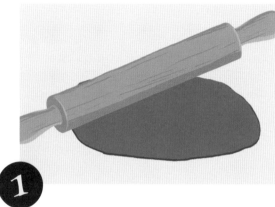

1 Spread out a plastic sheet or old tablecloth to work on. Work the clay in your hands to warm it. Roll out the blue clay until it's almost paper thin.

2 Take half the piece of red clay and roll it into a sausage about 1/4 inch in diameter.

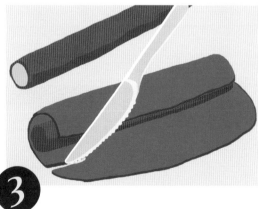

3 Put the red sausage on the blue piece and roll them up together. Now make a red sausage with a yellow middle in the same way.

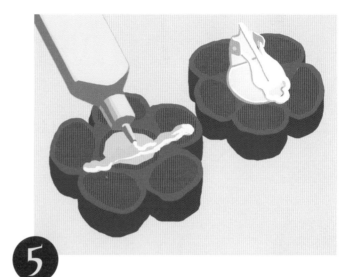

4 Cut the blue sausage into five equal pieces, and cut two equal piece of the red sausage. Arrange them in a flower shape as shown.

5 Use the plastic knife to slice the shape into two pieces. Bake them in the oven following the manufacturer's instructions. Leave them to cool, then glue the earring backs on.

Try This!

Pretty pendants
Once you get the hang of handling the clay, you can create all kinds of designs. Let your imagination run wild! These drop earrings were made with leftovers from the main project.

Bottle-top snake

Use the tops of plastic soft-drinks bottles to make a super, slithery snake. Ask an adult to save you the two wine corks you need.

You Will Need

- ✦ Champagne-style cork
- ✦ Wine cork
- ✦ Green acrylic paint and brush
- ✦ Plastic bottle tops: 30 green, a few red and white
- ✦ Old ballpoint pen
- ✦ 3 small screw eyes
- ✦ 24 inch string
- ✦ Small bell
- ✦ 2 googley eyes
- ✦ Scrap of red felt
- ✦ Scissors
- ✦ White glue

1 Paint the two corks all over with the green acrylic paint. Leave to dry.

2 Using the old ballpoint pen, make a hole in the middle of each of the bottle tops.

3 Screw one eye into the top of the champagne cork. Add the bell to another screw eye, and screw this and the remaining eye into each end of the wine cork.

4 Thread one end of the string through the bottom of a green bottle top. Now thread it though the champagne cork eye and back through the bottle top. Make a knot and trim one end only.

5 Thread all the bottle tops onto the string, keeping them all facing the same way round. Finish by tying the string to the screw eye on the wine cork.

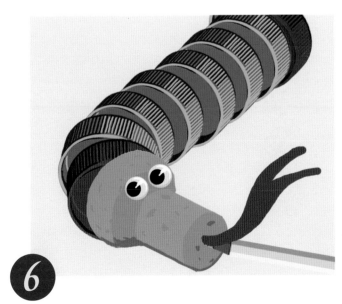

◀ Glue the two googley eyes in place. Cut a thin forked tongue from the red felt and use the pen to poke it into the cork.

6

Funky monkeys

This pair of acrobatic monkeys love just hanging around with each other! They are made from bendy pipe cleaners and fluffy pompoms.

You Will Need

- 3 x 12 inch brown chenille pipe cleaners
- White glue
- 4 x 2 inch pompoms
- 2 x 1 inch pompoms
- Scrap of beige felt
- Black fine marker pen
- 4 tiny goggle eyes

1 Cut the pipe cleaners in half to make 6 equal pieces. Bend one piece in half to make the legs, then bend the ends to make feet. Repeat with another piece for the arms and hands.

2 To make the tail, fix another pipe cleaner to the centre of the legs and arms, winding the end around at the bends to join them all together.

3 Use white glue to stick two of the larger pompoms together, sandwiching the legs, arms, and tail between them.

4 To make a head, cut a small figure-eight shape from the felt. Glue goggle eyes on the felt face and use the marker to draw nostrils and a mouth. Glue the face to a 1 inch pompom.

5 Glue the head to the top of the pompom body and leave it to dry. Bend the arms, legs, and tail into shape. Repeat for the second monkey.

Try This!

Creepy crawly

This terrifying tarantula is made from four pipe cleaners for the legs, with two pompoms holding them in place. Add eyes, antennas, and a hungry mouth and he'll give your friends the shivers!

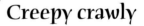

TOYS and GAMES

Tic-tac-toe game

Be green and save paper by making a tic-tac-toe game you can use over and over again!

You Will Need

- ✦ Foam: 1 sheet each in black, orange, purple, and green
- ✦ Sheet of thick cardboard 8 inch square
- ✦ Ruler
- ✦ Scissors
- ✦ White glue and brush
- ✦ Paper and pencil

1 Cut an 8 inch square of black funky foam and glue it to the sheet of thick cardboard.

2 Use the ruler and pencil to draw four strips on the orange foam, 8 inches long and about ¼ inch wide. Cut them out.

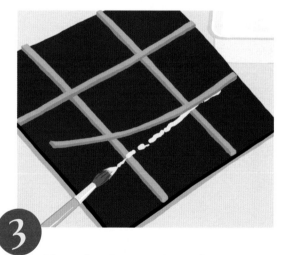

3 Glue the four strips of orange foam to the black foam in a criss-cross shape. You can use the ruler to help you position them evenly.

4 Cut the green funky foam in half and glue the halves together to make a double-thick sheet. Repeat with the purple foam.

5 Draw a large X and a 0 onto paper. Cut the shapes out and trace them onto the foam. Make five green X and five purple 0. Cut out the shapes, and you're ready to play!

Try This!

Shells and buttons

Instead of making your noughts and crosses, use shells and buttons to play with.

Cardboard car

Vroom! This car has proper wheels, so it will whizz along a smooth surface. You can use the card from an empty cereal box to make the body of the car.

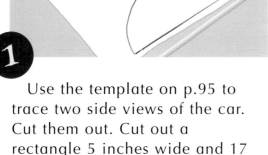

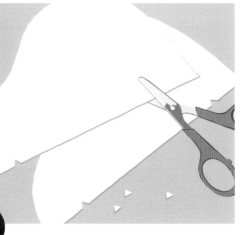

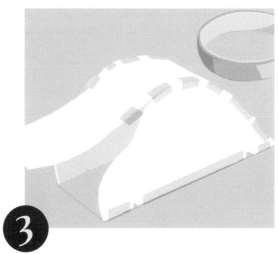

You Will Need

- ✦ Sheet of cardboard
- ✦ Scissors
- ✦ Masking tape
- ✦ Papier-mâché paste (see p.6)
- ✦ Old newspaper
- ✦ Sandpaper
- ✦ Set of paints and paintbrush
- ✦ 4 plastic bottle tops
- ✦ 2 straws
- ✦ 2 toothpicks

1 Use the template on p.95 to trace two side views of the car. Cut them out. Cut out a rectangle 5 inches wide and 17 inches long.

2 Snip out small V shapes 2 inches in from the ends of each side on both pieces of the car.

3 Tape all the pieces together. Cut a rectangle of cardboard to fit the base of the car and tape it on too.

70

4 Mix up some papier-mâché paste (see p.6) and tear up some newspaper. Cover the car in two layers of paper. Leave the model to dry.

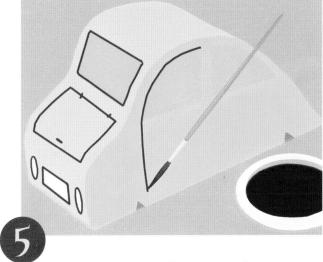

5 Rub the model all over with sandpaper. Paint your car yellow, then add windows, doors, a license plate, headlights, a driver, and a passenger.

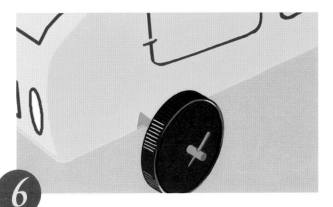

6 For wheels, make a hole in each bottle top. Push a straw through the hole and fix it with a small piece of a toothpick. Push the straw through to the other side, trim it to fit, and add the other wheel. Repeat for the back wheels.

71

Miniature theater

There's no need to be bored on a rainy day.
Make a shoe-box theater and get
your friends to help you
put on shows of your
favorite stories.

You Will Need

✦ Shoe box, about 12 x 10 inches
✦ Scissors
✦ Pencil, paints and brush
✦ White glue
✦ I yard red fabric
✦ Gold ribbon
✦ Wooden skewers
✦ Clear adhesive tape
✦ White paper
✦ Small square box
eg. raisin carton

1 Turn the box lengthways and cut a window in each side.

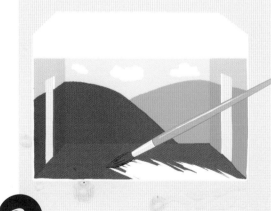

2 Draw a country scene of hills, sheep, and a blue sky with fluffy clouds on the back and sides. Color the scene with paints.

3 Cut two pieces of red fabric 16 x 8 inches. Glue them to the front of the box and decorate with gold ribbon. Cut a strip of fabric 31 inches long and cut one edge into a scalloped shape. Glue it along the top.

4 Draw a picture of Goldilocks and the Three Bears onto thick white paper. Paint them and leave them to dry.

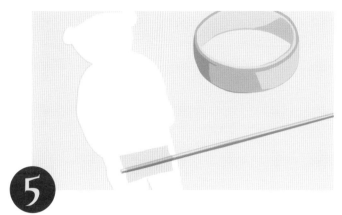

5 Cut out the characters and tape a wooden skewer to the back of each, near their feet.

◄ Make a table by cutting into a small cardboard package. Draw a blue checked tablecloth, cut it out and glue it to the table. Draw three porridge bowls and cut them out, leaving little tabs to stick them to the table.

6

Royal crown

Make a jeweled crown. Then decide, will you be a merry monarch or a rotten ruler?

You Will Need

- ✦ Strip of gold cardboard 5 x 24 inches
- ✦ 11 x 8 inch tracing paper and pencil
- ✦ Scissors and white glue
- ✦ Hologram film, 1 x 24 inches
- ✦ 2 strips of gold cardboard 1½ x 13 inches
- ✦ Paperclips and paper fastener
- ✦ Purple felt
- ✦ Large round plate
- ✦ Cotton batting
- ✦ Black paint and fine brush

1 Trace the the crown template on p.94. Transfer it onto the back of the gold cardboard, then repeat, butting the second section up to the first. Cut out the whole strip.

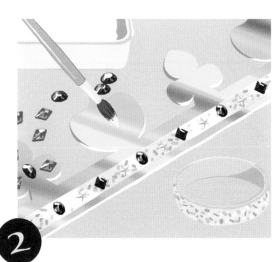

2 Glue the hologram film along the base, then glue gems along it and on the tops. Glue the two ends to fit loosely on your head, holding in place with paperclips.

Push a paper fastener through where the strips meet.

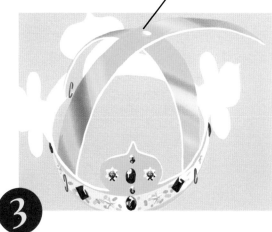

3 Make a mark halfway between the shapes. Glue the ends of the short gold strips over the marks. Hold them in place with paperclips while they dry.

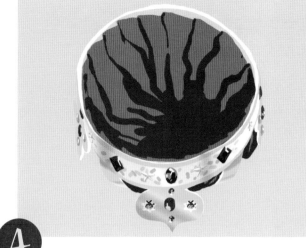

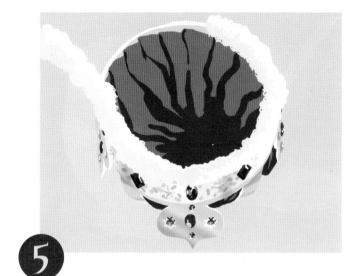

4 Trace around a dinner plate and cut out a circle of purple felt. Make small snips all around the outside of the circle. Put it inside the crown and glue to the inner brim, gluing bit by bit along the clipped edge.

5 Cut a strip of cotton batting about 2 inches wide. Glue it all along the bottom edge of the crown. Paint black spots about 1 inch apart along the length of the cotton batting.

Try This!

Top tiara

Make a simple tiara, cut out with pinking shears. Draw around a dinner plate onto the gold cardboard, then cut the it in half and glue it to a simple headband. Decorate the tiara with shiny foil and stick-on jewels.

Easter chick card

Take a break from devouring on your chocolate bunny to make a popup card. Chicks are traditional symbols of Easter. Try bluebirds for a birthday version.

You Will Need

+ 11 x 8 inch sheet of white cardboard
+ 11 x 8 inch sheet of orange cardboard
+ Scissors
+ White glue
+ Pencil
+ Felt-tipped pens or coloring pencils
+ Sheet of yellow paper

1 Fold both sheets of cardboard in half. Cut a $2\frac{1}{4}$ slit in the white card in the centre of the folded sheet, at right angles to the fold.

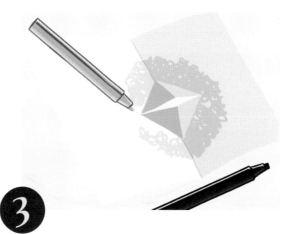

2 Carefully fold in both edges of the slit and make creases so that when you open and close the card, a beak shape pops out.

3 Draw a large, round chick's body around the beak shape. Use scribbly strokes to make your chick look fluffy.

4   Draw black eyes and legs on the body. Cut two wing shapes from the yellow paper and glue them to the body. Make sure the wings stay inside the edges of the card.

5   Paste glue over the back of the white card, avoiding the beak part. Stick it to the orange card, and write "Happy Easter" on the front of the card.

Try This!

Groovy chicks

Make a three-chick version by folding the card lengthways and cutting three slits for beaks.

Chinese dragon

Dragons are symbols of good fortune in Chinese New Year celebrations. Maybe this colorful dragon will bring you luck, so keep your fingers crossed!

You Will Need

✦ 11 x 8 inch colored paper: red, yellow, green
✦ Scissors
✦ White glue
✦ Clear adhesive tape
✦ Tissue paper: pink and white
✦ Pencil
✦ Paints: Black, red, yellow, gold, white
✦ Paintbrush
✦ Thick white paper
✦ Garden stakes

1 Cut the paper into 1½ inch wide strips and glue them together until you have two strips, each about 47 inches long.

2 Glue the two strips together at one end at right angles to each other. Put one strip over the other, folding it down. Repeat until the whole strip is folded.

3 Cut strips of pink and white tissue paper and attach them to one end of the strip for a tail.

4 Draw a dragon's head onto thick white paper. Cut it out and paint it yellow or orange with a red mouth.

5 Paint a big eye surrounded by circles, two nostrils, and black lips. Add gold highlights to the face. Make two fringes from the yellow and green papers and stick to the neck. Add pink tissue to the forehead.

6 Use clear adhesive tape to attach a garden stake to the back of the dragon's head. Add another near the tail and your dragon puppet is ready to roar!

Hanukkah candlestick

Jewish people celebrate the Hanukkah festival by lighting special candles and exchanging gifts. This special candlesholder is called a menorah.

1 Roll out the clay to ³/₄ inch. Put the template (see p.92) onto the clay and cut around it. On the flat end, using your toothpick, pierce nine small holes to mark the position of the candles.

You Will Need

✦ Tracing paper and pencil
✦ 18 ounces air-hardening clay
✦ Rolling pin
✦ Plastic knife
✦ Toothpick
✦ Ruler and old pen
✦ Gold paint and paintbrush
✦ 9 small candles

Make a mark on the pencil so you know how far down to push.

2 Push the end of the pencil about ¹/₂ inch into the holes. Do this for all except the middle hole which should only be 2 inches deep, so the candle will stand taller.

3 Roll out a small piece of clay and cut out a star using the template. Attach it to one side of the candlestick by wetting and scoring both pieces to help them stick.

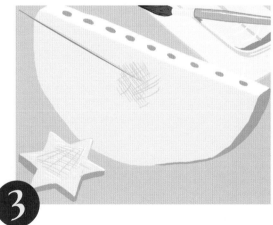

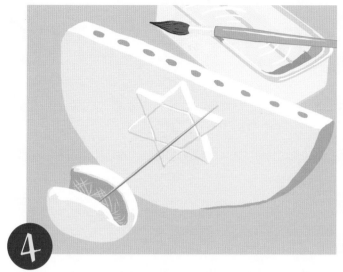

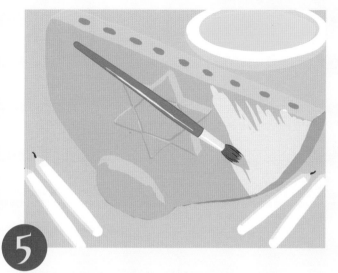

4 Roll a 2 inch ball of clay. Flatten the bottom and make a groove along the top. Stick it to the bottom of the candlestick. Make sure it stands firmly and leave it to dry.

5 Paint the candlestick gold all over and leave it to dry. Insert the nine candles into the candlestick holes and ask an adult to light them.

Halloween bat card

When you've finished trick-or-treating, make a spooky bat silhouette card for a really horrid halloween gift!

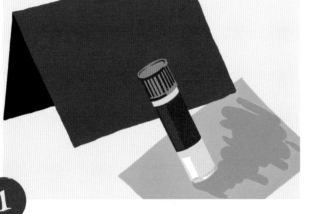

1 Fold the black card in half. Glue the orange paper to the front of the card, placing it centrally to leave a black border all around.

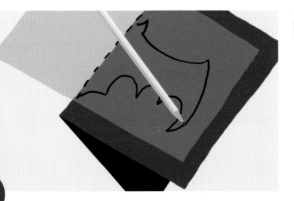

2 Trace the shape on p.93 onto tracing paper. Fold a sheet of black paper in half and put the tracing paper on top. Trace down the half-bat shape.

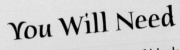

You Will Need

- ✦ 11 x 8 inch sheet of black cardboard
- ✦ Sheet of orange paper $4^3/_4$ x $7^1/_4$ inches
- ✦ Tracing paper and pencil
- ✦ 8 x 5 inch sheet black paper
- ✦ Scissors
- ✦ Gluestick
- ✦ 2 round green sequins

Top Tip

Trace marks can be difficult to see on the black paper. If you're good with scissors, cut out the bat instead. Line up the tracing paper so the edge of the bat is at the edge of the black paper. Grip both pieces of paper tightly and cut around the bat shape.

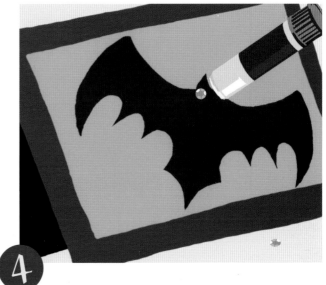

3 Cut out the half-bat, leaving the fold uncut. Open out the bat and apply glue over it. Stick it down at an angle on the front of the card.

4 Stick on green sequins with a dab of glue to add menacing bat's eyes.

Christmas stars

Are you in a hurry for Christmas? Make some sparkly foil tree decorations while you wait for the big day.

You Will Need

- ◆ Thick card
- ◆ Tracing paper and pencil
- ◆ Scissors
- ◆ White glue
- ◆ Foil candy wrappers
- ◆ Sequin stars
- ◆ Hole punch
- ◆ Gold cord

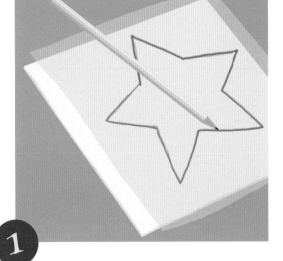

1 Trace the star from the template on p.92. Put the tracing on the card and draw over the lines to transfer it to the card.

2 Use the scissors to cut out the star design.

3 Tear the candy wrappers into small random pieces. Glue the pieces all over the star, overlapping them until the whole shape is covered. Leave to dry.

4 Glue sequin stars onto both sides of the foil-covered star. Leave to dry.

5 Use the hole punch to make a hole in one of the points of the star. Thread a length of gold cord through the hole and knot the ends together.

Try This!

Bells and trees
Make decorations in different shapes with a Christmas theme. You could try a green tree or a bell.

Nativity scene

This model looks beautiful and will help remind you of the wonderful story of the very first Christmas.

You Will Need

+ Packet of air-drying clay
+ Acrylic paints: red, yellow, blue, green, black, and gold
+ Small and medium paintbrushes

1

Make five thumb-shaped pieces of clay. These will be Mary, Joseph, and three shepherds. Make four sheep-shaped lumps. Make a small ball and press it in the middle to make a cradle. Flatten a tiny ball to make a baby that will fit in the cradle. Leave them to dry.

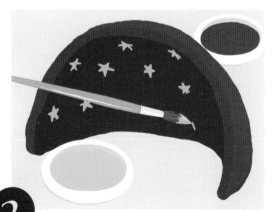

2

Roll out a fist-sized piece of clay and shape it into a cave. When it is hard and dry, paint the cave dark blue, with tiny gold stars all over the inside.

3

Paint Mary and Joseph, using a small brush. Give Mary a blue veil and Joseph a green robe. Wait for the paint to dry before adding the details on the faces.

Now paint the three shepherds with headdresses and bushy beards. Paint the sheep white, with black faces and feet.

4

5

Paint the cradle. Make the baby white, with black stripes to show that he is wrapped in a sheet. When it is dry, paint the baby's face and features.

Try This!

Three Kings

Add the Three Kings to your Christmas scene. Paint gold details on their clothes to make them look grand.

Mother's Day photo booklet

Your Mom will love to keep her favorite pictures of you in this cool photo album.

You Will Need

✦ 2 pieces of thick card 6in x 6in
✦ 2 sheets A4 purple paper
✦ Sticky tape
✦ White glue
✦ 1 metre turquoise ribbon
✦ Sheet of turquoise paper 6in x 24in
✦ Pencil and ruler
✦ Blue corrugated card 4in x 4in
✦ Small square of purple felt
✦ Zig-zag scissors
✦ Gems to decorate

1 Wrap each sheet of purple paper around a square of cardboard and fix in place with clear adhesive tape.

2 Cut the ribbon into four equal strips. Glue to the back of the purple cards, as shown above. Trim the end of each ribbon into a V shape.

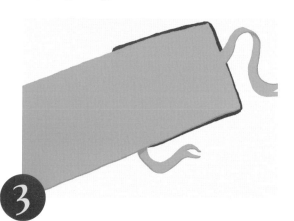

3 Glue the end of the sheet of turquoise paper to the wrong side of one of the purple boards.

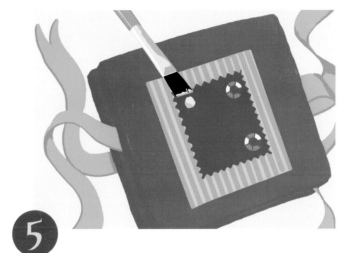

4 Fold the turquoise paper strip three times, accordian-style. Glue the last fold to the wrong side of the remaining purple board.

5 Decorate the front by sticking on some blue corrugated cardboard, then a smaller square of purple felt cut with zig-zag scissors. Glue some gems to the felt as a finishing touch.

Cut triangles from purple felt to fix the corners of your photos in place.

Halloween lantern

Halloween would not be complete without a glowing jack-o-lantern. Put one in your window to greet trick-or-treaters.

You Will Need

- ◆ Medium-sized pumpkin
- ◆ Spoon or ice-cream scoop
- ◆ Felt-tipped pen
- ◆ Small knife
- ◆ Short, fat candle

1 Scoop out the insides of the pumpkin, using a spoon or an ice-cream scoop.

2 Use a felt-tipped pen to draw a scary face onto the pumpkin.

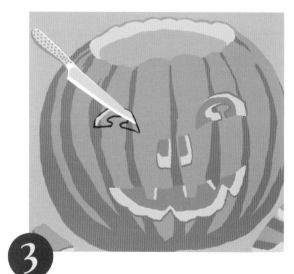

3 Now for the tricky part! Ask an adult to cut away the marked pattern, using a small knife.

4

Put a small candle inside the pumpkin and ask an adult to light it.

Try This!

Scary cat

You can make all kinds of faces on your pumpkin. This spooky witch's cat uses the stalk as a nose. Great idea!

Top Tip

If your pumpkin dries out and looks withered, soak it in cold water for a few hours and it will be as good as new.

Top templates

Draw round these shapes with a pencil onto tracing paper, then turn the tracing paper over lay on plain paper and scribble over the lines.

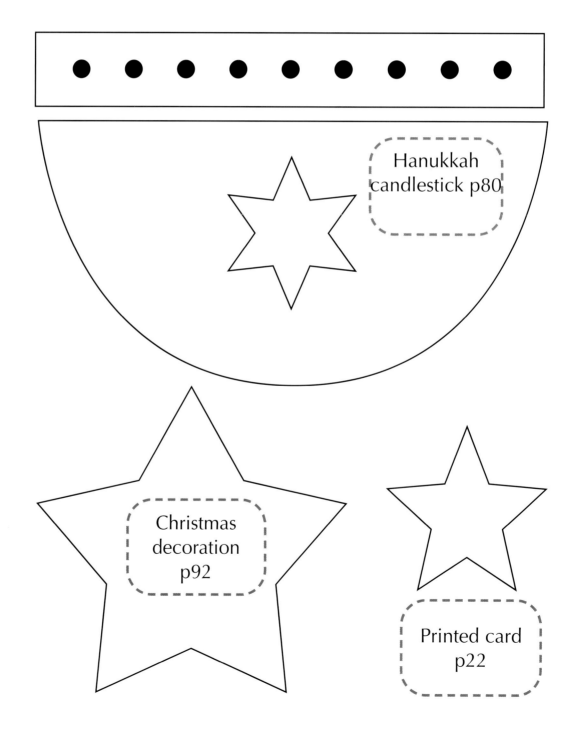

Hanukkah candlestick p80

Christmas decoration p92

Printed card p22

Halloween bat
card
p.82

Dinosaur
mail holder
p. 24

Royal crown
p.74

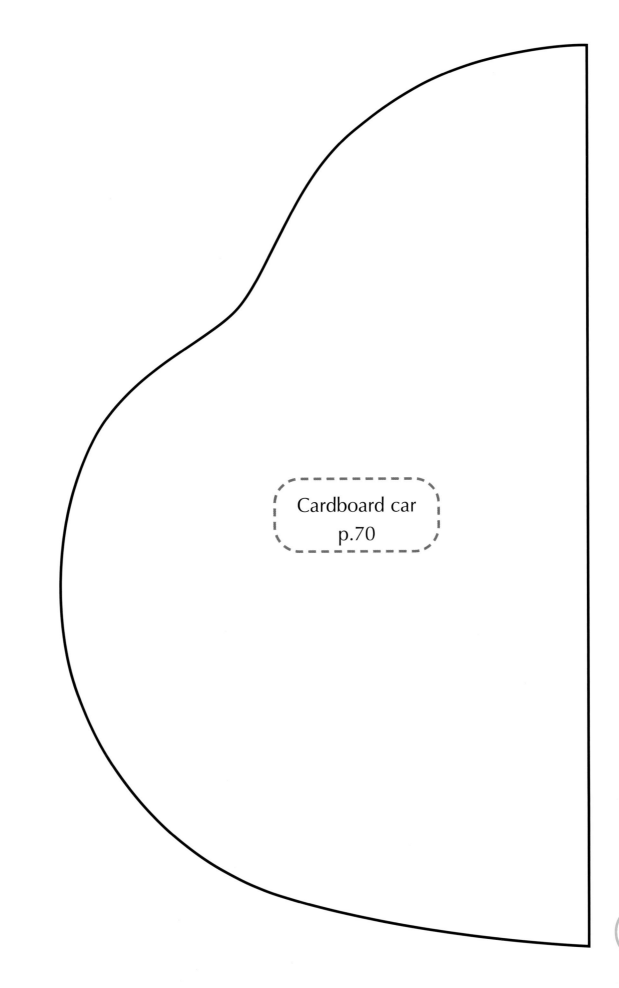

Cardboard car
p.70

Index

Credits

Project creators: Anita Ruddell
Melanie Williams
Illustrator: Gary Walton

Photographer: John Englefield
Project editor: Rona Skene
Produced by DropCap Ltd